THE
FROG BROTHERS
EDGAR & ALAN
EST. 1987
VAMPIRE HUNTERS
SANTA CARLA, CA
"If you try to stop us, or vamp out in any way, we'll stake you without even thinking twice about it!"